WHEN
IT HURTS TOO MUCH TO
LET GO

Where to Find Hope, Healing, and Wellness

WHEN
IT HURTS TOO MUCH TO
LET GO

Where to Find Hope, Healing, and Wellness

KETSIA MORAND

ISBN: 978-1-7777865-0-2
Legal deposit: August 2021.
Bibliothèque et Archives nationales du Québec
Bibliothèque et Archives nationales du Canada

Contents

Preface

I am not presenting myself as a psychologist or a therapist. I am simply a woman who had an encounter with God during a dark chapter of her life. I then understood that, in order to heal, I had to fill my brain with the proper knowledge, perspective, and perceptions.

I had to seek an understanding of the Word of God to break free from the repeated cycles in my life. I also had to dig deeper within myself to understand why I was constantly getting a certain outcome. Finally, I had to understand the countless feelings I was experiencing and identify the barriers holding me back from emotional healing.

Overcoming various hardships in the past has led me to believe a part of my calling is to help people who are stagnant in their healing process. I wrote this book to help others build confidence and find spiritual, mental, and physical balance.

Acknowledgments

First of all, I would like to thank God for making this project possible.

I want to thank my friend, Rosie Aworie, who was the first one who pushed me to write this book. She believed in me when I did not believe that this project was possible.

I would like to thank Coach Katherine Clerdonna. Thank you for the great coaching and priceless pieces of advice you provided me. You gave me life and gave me all the tools I needed to succeed—you are the best.

I want to thank my daughter, Eden, and my husband, GG. You supported me throughout the whole process. I love you, you are the best, and you make my world better every day.

I would like to thank my parents, my brothers, my sisters, and my in-laws. I do not know what I would do without you guys. I love you.

I want to thank my prayer sisters, Francesca, Kathy, Stephanie, Scarlene, Maddana, Lidy, and Naisha—may God bless you, girls! Thank you for being shoulders and incredible prayer partners.

I want to thank Rosie Aworie, Romel Slyne, Greg & Liberty, Ilze Lyell, Savannah M., Rachelle Jacques, and Les éditions blossom for helping me edit this book and ensuring its excellence.

I would like to thank Svitlana Stefaniuk for the book cover. You did a fantastic job. I love it! Thank you for putting all your heart into it. You nailed it!

Not least, I would like to thank you for getting this book. May God help you reach the wellness goal you desire to achieve. Be blessed.

Ketsia Morand

Introduction

Have you ever found yourself so deeply emotionally hurt that you felt like there is no way out of that predicament?

Or maybe you keep finding yourself in the same compromising situations, repeatedly, even though you know they are toxic for your well-being. Yet, you are unable to take the necessary steps to break free. Perhaps you are emotionally ill right now, feeling lost and confused, thinking that all hope is gone. Or maybe you have been so overwhelmed by hardships that you have faith for others, but not for yourself.

If any of the statements mentioned resemble your current situation, then this book is for you. In fact, this book is for anyone who has tried everything they could to heal and has not yet succeeded.

Being unable to let go can be an overwhelming feeling. My mission is to show you who, or what, the real culprit is. Repeated patterns come from our mental perspectives, which are often fed by obstacles and lies we hold in our minds. Well, I have great news for you: complete healing is possible, and you can have it!

This book is not meant to be used as a replacement for professional counseling or therapy, but more as a guide to kickstart your journey toward healing and wellness.

With the help of the Holy Spirit, and by understanding what lies are holding you back, I believe you will be able to reach a new dimension of freedom, one you have never known before.

At the end of each chapter, you will find prayers, Bible verses, and questions to help you dig deeper and reach your daily meditation goals.

Chapter 1

It All Starts in Our Minds

We must understand our brains,
our minds, and our behavior.

After being left by a man whom she considered to be the love of her life, Naomie found herself depressed, confused, and filled with a deep emotional pain that she could not understand. Unable to function or focus on mundane tasks, such as doing homework, cleaning, having simple conversations, or anything else that would require energy, Naomie felt lost.

Eventually, she dropped out of school, quit her job, and could only find comfort in her favorite isolated place: her bed.

What was wrong with Naomie? Why was she so profoundly hurt and paralyzed by that grief?

Why did she feel as if her life was over? After all, it was just a breakup, as many would say.

Why do we sometimes remain stuck in our hardships?

Why is it so hard to let go? Why is it so hard to get over painful situations? To answer these questions, we must understand how the mind functions.

"According to the National Institute of Mental Health, more than 30 million Americans need help dealing with feelings and problems related

to marriage, relationships, family situation, losing a job, the death of a loved one, depression, stress, burnout, or substance abuse." [1]

It is normal to be affected by life circumstances, but when these situations become overwhelming and cause problems beyond our control, it is a sign of an issue that must be dealt with.

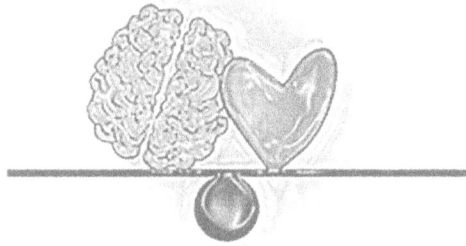

The Mind

We cannot discuss the mind without considering the brain. Most of the time, these two words are used interchangeably. However, they are different in many ways.

The brain is like a computer hard drive, and the mind, a computer software. We can also compare the brain to a recording machine and the mind to the tape-recording data. Globally speaking, the human brain is a fascinating organ identified as a physical, visible, and tangible place in our heads.

This brilliant organ is known to be the control center of the nervous system and is responsible for the coordination of the movements and responses of our bodies.

---

[1] "How to Choose a Psychologist," American Psychology Association, October 17, 2019, www.apa.org/helpcenter/choose-therapist.

On the other hand, the mind is invisible. It is associated with our emotions, feelings, thoughts, concepts, beliefs, and emotional intelligence.

It is safe to say that the mind is the active area of the head, where the brain is the organ, and the mind functions through that organ. In summary, we can say that the mind refers to a person's understanding and conscience.

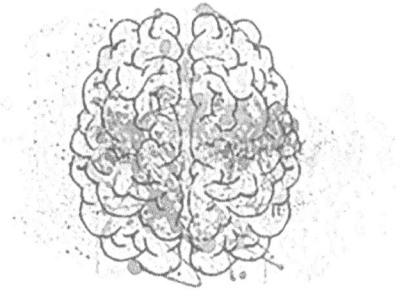

My goal is not to get into too many biological notions, but to help you understand the interaction between the brain, mind, emotions, and behaviors. Understanding these interactions will facilitate your emotional healing. And emotional healing will allow you to let go, make peace with the circumstances that negatively affected you, and regain control of your feelings, mind, thoughts, and behavior.

The Brain, The Mind, and Our Behavior

Why do we react differently to and have different perceptions of the same events? Why do the same conditions create varying emotions in each of us?

Why do some people seem to be more affected by their circumstances than others? Throughout my diligent pursuit to answer these questions, I realized that our interpretation of an event determines the emotions we feel, not the situation itself.

Since everyone's emotional associations with life events are different, it is reasonable to say feelings and understandings are subjective from one person to another. Many factors influence how we think and what we understand from life circumstances. Some of those factors could be our childhood, our past experiences, or simply the state of mind we are in at the moment of the event.

How you respond to an event reveals a lot about how you perceived said situation. For example, you might respond with anger, if you believe what happened to you is unjustified or that others are to blame. You might react with shame, if you think the situation revealed a shortcoming. You might respond with sadness or guilt, if you think about the negative consequences the event or "failure" will have on others or yourself. You might reply with or maintain positive emotions, if you think you have done what was right and that what went wrong is not your responsibility at all. [2]

Like Naomie, you might feel defeated if the man who left you meant the world to you, and you feel like you will not be able to overcome the loss. On the other hand, someone else might be sad because of a breakup but confident that they will find the right person at the right time.

Once again, it is not only the situation we face that determines how we feel but also how we interpret the situation. This is because our brains are remarkably in sync with our minds.

---

[2] Matthias Siemer, Iris Mauss, and James Gross, "Same Situation-Different Emotions: How Appraisals Shape Our Emotions," Emotion (Washington, D.C.) 7 (September 1, 2007): 592–600, https://doi.org/10.1037/1528-3542.7.3.592.

They are like two superheroes working in close collaboration. Our brains take in information from life events and give them meaning through cognitive and non-conscious analysis. As a result, we experience emotions, feelings and eventually develop reasoning and critical judgment.

It is crucial to understand that our thoughts reinforce our behavior and guide us in the decisions we make. For example, have you ever noticed how often we have conversations with ourselves before making decisions?

To understand the relationship between thoughts, feelings, and actions, let's take a look at the cognitive triangle theory.

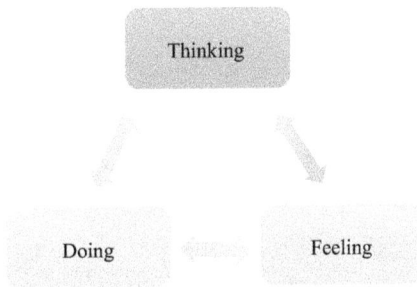

Thinking

Doing   Feeling

The Cognitive Triangle Theory

The cognitive triangle is a successful pictogram based on the theoretical model of psychologists, Albert Ellis and Aaron Beck. This concept is a successful tool used in CBT (Cognitive Behavioral Therapy), created to help us understand the interaction between external events, perceptions, thoughts, feelings, and actions.

This theory stands on the belief that, once you change your thinking, you can change your emotions and behavior. We will examine this concept further in the following chapter. For now, it is essential to remember that the brain receives information from the external world through our five senses—sight, hearing, smell, touch, and taste—and then gives them meaning through the trilogy of the mind, which is cognition, affection, and conation—also called the thinking, feeling, and doing parts.

The Trilogy of the Mind: Cognition, Affection, and Conation

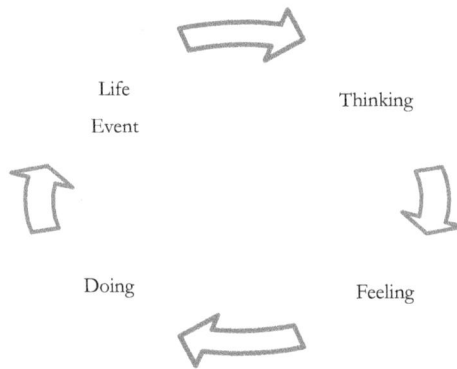

Life Event

Thinking

Doing

Feeling

To recognize the trilogy of the mind in your everyday thought process, here are three questions you can ask yourself:

1. *What is going on?*
2. *How does this make me feel?*
3. *What should I do?*

1. Thinking part of the mind : Cognition (What is going on?)

Cognition is the mental process of acquiring understanding through our thoughts. It is the part where we analyze external information through our minds. This process is what gives meaning to events and allows an understanding of our situation.

2. Feeling part of the mind 😃: Affection (How does this make me feel?)

Affection is the feeling that causes us to be affected by events. Our thoughts create feelings, emotions, and beliefs, eventually leading us to make decisions.

3. Doing part of the mind 🏃 : Conation (What should I do?)

Conation is the will to act. Based on a subjective judgment led by our emotions, we make decisions and choose our actions. As a result, our behavior reinforces our thoughts, and the cycle continues.

> Cognition: Is the mental process of acquiring understanding through thought.
>
> Affection: Are the feelings which affect us.
>
> Conation: Is the mental faculty of purpose, desire or will to perform an action.

Everything we go through, from childhood to this day, affects us in so many ways. All our experiences are stored in different layers of our consciousness.

Therefore, when facing new situations, our minds react based on the recollection of old emotions and memories.

However, we must be aware that our mind's interpretation based on recalled information is not always accurate.

Let's take, for example, people who went through emotional or psychological trauma. Based on an ongoing, or one-time, stressful event, they can see almost anything as a potential danger or source of extreme anxiety.

These types of mind connections are common in people who went through a car accident, resulting in being afraid of driving again; humiliation, resulting in isolation and low self-esteem; or the sudden death of a loved one, resulting in being afraid of having significant connections with people for fear of becoming too attached, and losing them at some point. This is one of the ways cognitive distortions can be created.

The misconceptions of the traumatizing events that our brains create blur our perceptions. In return, our minds convince us of things that are not true. Subsequently, these inaccurate thoughts reinforce a negative way of feeling and thinking, causing stored information from our past to affect our beliefs and everyday behavior.

> The action we adopt represents our behavior. Now, if we had to describe the word behavior in a simple word, it is the way one conducts oneself in response to a situation or stimulus.
>
> They are influenced by our perceptions, understanding, and beliefs.

Our Beliefs and the Three Levels of Awareness

When discussing behaviors and beliefs, there are three levels of consciousness: the conscious mind, the subconscious mind, and the unconscious mind.

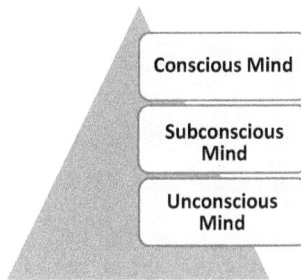

The conscious mind is the sphere in which we are aware of what is happening around us and inside us. It is what generates an immediate reaction from us, such as hitting the brakes after realizing that another car just cut us off.

It uses information from our external environment, along with our memories, through the subconscious mind.

The subconscious mind acts as a storehouse. It contains all our experiences, our memories, and a buildup of ideas created throughout our lifetime. It is where information can either be stored or brought back into the conscious mind whenever required. It is what helps us remember how to do the things that we have learned. For instance, when we say that we are on autopilot, it is the subconscious mind that helps us to do the tasks without much thought, such as remembering our phone number, driving our way back home from work, remembering how to write, and so on. Everything we go through in our lives is stored and processed there.

It is also where the mind gathers information from previous experiences, associates them with general life events, and consequently impacts our everyday decisions and behaviors. That is the level of awareness at which the interpretation of our experiences occurs without us even being aware of it.

The unconscious mind, on its own, is also a storehouse. Therefore, the significant difference between the subconscious and the unconscious is that the unconscious mind contains the repressed memories and past experiences that we cannot recollect.

There can be different factors that cause us to repress events from our memories. For example, emotional trauma, physical trauma, or simply forgetting non-meaningful events or things that are no longer important to us, such as childhood memories, an old house address, or postal code.

I cannot stress enough how much events and repressed memories, even when no longer remembered, still affect our present life. The conscious mind is in constant communication with the subconscious, and the unconscious reinforces the subconscious mind. However, I have great news for you. Now that we are aware of the dimensions of the mind, beliefs, and repressed memories, we can implement intentional thinking in our everyday lives to experience significant changes and positive results.

While some people choose to rely on hypnotic techniques to help them affect these changes, I recommend prayer and meditation of the word of God, instead. God, who knows everything, will give you the revelation that you need about your past, to understand and help you reprogram your mind, thoughts, habits, and beliefs.

As a reminder, I would like to equip you with four keys that will help you achieve an authentic recovery:

☞ **The primary key** for an authentic recovery and a faster healing process is to make the unconscious conscious through prayer. God knows everything. Never forget that it is God's plan for your life that you heal emotionally. He wants, even more than you do, to see you emotionally well. He wants to reveal to you all the life events that are still affecting you negatively.

☞ **The second key** to an authentic recovery is to avoid isolating yourself. It is okay to ask for help. Prayer is fantastic, but seeking a good Christian therapist and prayer partner to help you through the process is important, as well. God did not create us to be alone. That is why we have the body of Christ, a community of people with whom we can connect, support, and help one another overcome hardships.

☞ **The third key** for an authentic recovery is to not let the judgment of others determine who you are. You must get to know your true self and where you are going. Along the way, you might find people trying to make you feel weak for still being affected by situations that happened years ago, or maybe identifying you by the mistakes you made in your past.

You may think that this is going to be a long process, that it might take forever. However, I want to encourage you to pursue the journey step-by-step, one day at a time. Healing occurs every step of the way. Feeling better, and stronger, occurs consistently for the one who seeks that healing. Every step of the journey improves one's life, even when addressing the challenges brings out emotions. There is so much freedom in that healing. Thankfully, we are never alone in this process. God is willing to help us.

⚷ **The Fourth and Last Key** for an authentic recovery is to not compare yourself with others. Pain is relative, and we do not experience it the same way. Additionally, we are all different, and it is only normal that each and every one of us advances at our own pace.

Let Us Pray!

Dear God, what are the experiences that are negatively influencing and polluting my mind? What is holding me back from moving forward? Heavenly Father, help me to see clearly; reset my mind, and reprogram me to the way you first intended me to be.
It is in the mighty name of Jesus Christ that I pray.
Amen!

Meditation Verses

The Bible tells us:

Hebrews 4:12 (NIV)

For the word of God is alive and active. Sharper than any double-edged sword, it penetrates even to dividing soul and spirit, joints, and marrow; it judges the thoughts and attitudes of the heart.

Romans 12:2 (NLT)

Do not copy the behavior and customs of this world, but let God transform you into a new person by changing the way you think. Then you will learn to know God's will for you, which is good and pleasing and perfect.

Philippians 4:6-7 (NKJV)

Be anxious for nothing, but in everything by prayer and supplication, with thanksgiving, let your requests be made known to

God; and the peace of God, which surpasses all understanding, will guard your hearts and minds through Christ Jesus.

Isaiah 26:3 (NLT)

You will keep in perfect peace all who trust in you, all whose thoughts are fixed on you!

Psalm 119:165 (NKJV)

Great peace have those who love Your law, and nothing causes them to stumble.

1 Corinthians: 1:8 (NIV)

He will also keep you firm to the end, so that you will be blameless on the day of our Lord Jesus Christ.

Philippians 1:6 (NIV)

Being confident of this, that he who began a good work in you will carry it on to completion until the day of Christ Jesus.

Study Questions

1. How does your mind hinder you from moving forward?

   _____

   _____

   _____

2. How have memories and past events affected you so far?

   _____

   _____

   _____

3. What practical things can you do to start renewing your mind?

   _____

   _____

   _____

Notes

Chapter 2

The Predispositions and Factors

We Must Identify the Root Causes of Our Circumstances.

Nursing and medical schools train their students to recognize pathologies by observing the signs and symptoms felt by their patients. Before prescribing any treatment, they must first determine what is going on within the patient. For example, is this headache a result of a blood circulation issue, or is it caused by other factors? We can only address a problem effectively by identifying its root cause. For example, cutting down a tree does not guarantee that the soil will not be affected. It must be uprooted.

> "You can only treat a problem once you have been able to identify its root cause."

Some trees remain alive underneath the ground even when it is cut at its trunk. Therefore, to be killed, these trees must be unrooted.

The same thing goes with our lives. We go through situations that, even when no longer occurring, still affect us years later, causing deep damage inside of us. This happens if the root cause has not been dealt with.

We Must Bring to Light What is Holding Us Back

After realizing that we are emotionally affected, recognizing what is holding us back from healing is essential. It could be a spiritual hindrance, emotional baggage, a hormonal imbalance, a mental illness such as anxiety, or some other cause preventing us from moving forward. Since each problem does not require the same treatment, we must identify the type of giants we face if we want to receive proper help. Conversely, receiving the wrong treatment will only prolong our journey to wellness.

It is okay to get help to demystify all of this. Trying to figure it out alone can be overwhelming, and that is why there are professionals available to assist you in the process.

> We live in an era where everything is accessible through the internet, which could be an excellent tool. Therefore, we must be careful: a lack of knowledge and training can sometimes have us wrongly self-diagnose our self.
>
> That is why, when it comes to our physical, mental, and spiritual health, diagnosis should always be made by a certified professional or a spiritual leader.

To help you recognize the possible root causes of what is hindering you from achieving wellness, you will find a list of the most common factors that can hinder a person's wellness journey.

But, before we continue, let's pray!

Heavenly Father,
Forgive us for our shortcomings.
You know us better than anyone else.
We need Your help in demystifying what is hindering us from being well.
We need Your help and guidance to be prepared for what is coming.
Open our eyes and heart to the healing You desire to do in us.
Please give us Your spirit of understanding and discernment.
Thank You for the restoration that You are about to bring in our lives.
It is in the mighty name of Jesus Christ that we pray.
Amen!

Fasten your seat belt. Are you ready to start your wellness journey?

While going through this chapter, I encourage you to do a self-analysis and jot down the things that resonate with you. Remember, being aware of the obstructions in your life allows you to build a better and more mindful strategy for emotional healing.

These are general factors, so I encourage you to do an in-depth assessment that applies to your situation.

Mental Health

I pray that the stigmas of mental illness and the belief that Christians should not consult therapists will be broken. Mental illnesses affect us in so many ways and to different degrees. For so long, religion has allowed misconceptions about mental health and is known to consider mental and emotional illnesses to stem from demonic influence.

"There is freedom on the other side of fear."

People affected by illnesses are not necessarily possessed by demons. Unfortunately, for far too long, people have been suffering because of this misconception, bound with the fear of being judged. The opposite is also true: many people receive medications for things that should be dealt with on a spiritual level.

To identify what type of hindrances we are experiencing, discernment and the assistance of the Holy Spirit is strongly needed.

When searching for a life coach, therapist, or counselor, the things you should look for are professionalism, a qualified person in the sphere you need help, a person whose faith and values match your own, and a person who preserves your confidentiality. The last thing you want is to have your personal situation circulating in the street or social media without your consent.

☹ Fear: False Evidence Appearing Real

Fear is the number one factor that holds most people back and prevents them from recovering. It is an emotion generated by something, or someone, we identify as a threat, and that may cause us harm. This may influence our behavior, as a result.

> "When fear informs our behaviors,
> it sabotages our fruitfulness and
> truthfulness."
> Jackie Hill-Perry

Some of the most common types of fears are the fear of being alone, fear of losing, fear of failing, fear of being judged, fear of rejection, fear of not being loved, and the list goes on. Nourished by our past, our thoughts, and the unrealistic stories we tell ourselves, fear develops in the restrictions of our life.

It paralyzes our minds and creates a strong sense of apprehension.

It blurs our capacity to see clearly, undermines our real abilities, and creates an inaccurate perspective of life.

Love versus Fear

Love and fear are on opposite ends of a spectrum of emotions. Therefore, we cannot be on the frequency of fear and love at the same time.

The Bible also talks about these two opposite frequencies. For instance, the book of 1 John 4:18 tells us: "God is love, and that perfect love casts out fear."

I believe the love and presence of God cannot be neglected when achieving complete wellness.

> Love attracts the following:
> Patience, joy, peace, compassion, sacrifice, healthy relational attachments, healing, fullness, wholesomeness, and caring behaviors.
> Fear attracts the following:
> Worry, impatience, clinginess, emotional disorders, insecurities, manipulation, depression, loneliness, and psychological-protection mechanisms.

When fear remains unaddressed, it inevitably opens doors to other complications, such as developing certain personality traits that make us more vulnerable to experiencing negativity and toxicity.

> "There is no fear in love. But perfect love drives out fear because fear has to do with punishment. The one who fears is not made perfect in love."
> 1 John 4:18 NIV

The two most common traits birthed by fear are insecurities in the form of *emotional dependency* and *low self-esteem*.

😟 Emotional Dependency

It is normal to be attached to the people whom we love. However, a sign of an underlying problem is when one experiences constant fear of losing people, sometimes for no apparent reason.

We often hear about emotional dependency without having a clear understanding of what it is. As a result, many people are not aware that they suffer from it.

As of May 22, 2019, the *Collins English Dictionary* defined dependency as the situation in which you need something or someone all the time, especially to continue existing or operating. We can also characterize emotional dependency as emotional distress and insecure attachments to other people.

According to Dr. Steve Bressert, a dependent personality disorder is characterized by a long-standing need to be taken care of by someone, and a fear of being abandoned or separated from individuals considered important in one's life. This behavior will lead the person to engage in a dependent and submissive behavior designed to provoke caregiving behaviors in others. The addicted person may be seen as being "clingy" or "clinging onto" others because the person cannot live without the help or presence of others.

Low Self-Esteem

Low self-esteem is a subjective self-appreciation. It is a debilitating condition that keeps individuals from realizing their full potential. It refers to an individual's opinion of their self-value, making the person affected feel unworthy, incapable, and incompetent of doing anything without seeking the approval of others.

The general signs of low self-worth are a constant fear of not being adequate, always seeking external validation, lack of boundaries, a constant feeling of being defeated, feelings of shame, pessimism, feeling the need to compare to others, and putting other people first, even when it is toxic for oneself.

Affective dependency and low self-esteem represent the most common obstructions to human well-being. However, when we gain self-confidence and learn how to overcome our fears by trusting God, we increase in strength.

As we saw in the previous chapter, most of the time, fears are nourished by lies or misconceptions that our mind believes to be true.

Lies & Strongholds

Lies perpetuate false beliefs in our lives. Since our beliefs represent our reality, whether our conclusions are factual or not, what we believe becomes our guideline, not to mention that lies create limitations, heaviness, depression, and confusion.

Lies make us think things will never get better, forcing us to stay in our comfort zones.

Like faith, lies come from what we hear. This can happen through a negative inner voice or by accepting false claims made by other people. As a result, just as a seed grows in the ground, these false beliefs become more prominent and confine us within strongholds.

A stronghold is defined as a fortified, strong-walled fortress. It refers to our reasoning, reinforced with lies that distort our thinking, logic, personality, and perception.

These fortresses are known to cause emotional, spiritual, and behavioral issues. An extension of strongholds is cognitive distortions.

Cognitive distortion

Generally unconscious, cognitive distortions are beliefs, or thoughts, that give us an inaccurate vision of reality. It is a misconception, a condition that alters our view of the world, how we see others, and how we see ourselves. Furthermore, it creates unhealthy relationships and interactions, negative emotions, and untruthful thoughts.

There are more than 50 types of cognitive distortions, with the following 12 being the most common:

1. Always Being Right

The belief that we must always be correct, the thought that we know the absolute truth; this is when the concept of being wrong is not conceivable.

2. Blaming

Blaming other people, or blaming ourselves, for our issues, even when it has nothing to do with us, and holding other people accountable for our pain.

For example, telling someone that gave us a negative comment, "You make me feel bad," while, in fact, it is the perspective we have of their criticism and the acceptance of the comment as the truth that made us feel bad.

3. Catastrophizing (minimizing or exaggerating)

It is the exaggeration of insignificant events. For example, a great musician is missing a note during a big show. Even though no one notices, he magnifies his mistake and starts to believe he is a terrible musician, convincing himself that his life is over because of that mistake.

Catastrophizing distortion can also manifest in the form of minimizing the magnitude of an event. For instance, a person receives an award for excellent work but persists in believing that they are not intelligent and did not deserve the honorable mention.

4. Control Fallacies

This misconception leads one to believe they have no control over their lives or see themselves as victims of fate. This can also be identified as believing that we are in control of ourselves and others. It can be described as feeling responsible for how others think, or assuming that we are responsible for the sadness or happiness of people around us.

For example, a co-worker seems to be in a bad mood, and we automatically assume that we must have wronged him somehow, causing him to be in that mood.

5. Emotional Reasoning

Emotional reasoning is identified as seeing emotions as truth. It manifests through confusing our "distorted emotions" with reality taking one's feelings as fact. You can recognize this distortion when the assumption is made that "I feel that way, so it must be true."

For example, I feel healthy, so I must not be sick.

6. The Fallacy of Fairness

It is the misconception that we live in a fair world.

People living with this distortion are most likely to experience disappointments, frustrations, discouragement, anger, resentment, and hopelessness when they experience the unfairness of life. We must understand that, while we serve a fair God, we do not live in a fair world.

7. Filtering

This distortion is a mental filter that causes us to only focus on the negative, excluding the positive.

For instance, a person only focuses on what they do wrong, on one single negative thing that occurs, or only the negative comments that are made.

8. Jumping to Conclusions

This revolves around assuming we know what other people think. It is a negative interpretation of what we think other people have in mind. It is the belief that we can read other people's minds. It can be manifested by jumping to the conclusion that our future is pre-set to our present situation.

For example, a single woman who thinks that she will never find a great partner or get married because she is still single. Or believing that a breakup means she won't ever find someone again.

9. Overgeneralizing

Generalizing one fact to encompass other scenarios that were not affected by this one instance.

For example, a student, who fails an exam, concludes that he is a failure and not intelligent. This distortion is manifested by false-negative facts based on a single experience.

10. Personalization

Taking everything personally. Turning what other people say and do into a personal insult, even when it has nothing to do with us. Relating unconnected external events to us.

11. Polarized Thinking

This is black or white thinking; an all-or-nothing mentality, or the inability to balance things. It is an "either/or" mindset.

For example, something is either great or a mess. It is either a success or a failure. In this distortion category, the person only sees the extremes.

12. Should Statements

This distortion can be manifested by a person imposing rigid guidelines on themselves or others. When these strict guidelines are not met, it makes the person feel angry, guilty, and frustrated. You can recognize this distortion when a person is inclined to use the words *should, must, have to, need to,* and so on.

> "It is not about what you say, but it's more about what you believe in, that will be your guideline."

Strongholds withhold us from being free. These distortions thrive in untreated emotional wounds, disappointment, and pride.

Recognizing Strongholds

One thing that may help recognize strongholds in our life is the continuous belief that it is impossible to get better spiritually despite so many attempts to change.

You pray and pursue God but still experience a strong resistance toward real spiritual change. After a sincere pursuit of God, you find it hard to believe the Word of God, and you experience a strong and steady feeling of confusion and rebellion against God and His recommendations.

If you fall into this category where you feel imprisoned by fortified blocks, I have good news for you! Be encouraged. Strongholds are breakable through prayer. Besides, now that you are more aware of what strongholds are, you will be able to direct your prayers in the right direction.

To help you in this process, I have included an example of prayer at the end of this chapter. The prayer has been worded to inspire you on how to pray to break strongholds. Therefore, I want you to know that there is no recipe for a perfect prayer except for using the assistance of the Holy Spirit. So, let Him guide you while you pray.

> "For though we walk in the flesh, we do not war according to the flesh. For the weapons of our warfare are not carnal but mighty in God for pulling down strongholds."
> 2 Corinthians 10:3-4 (NKJV)

> "Do not conform to the pattern of this world but be transformed by the renewing of your mind. Then you will be able to test and approve what God's will is—his good, pleasing, and perfect will."
> Romans 12:2 (NIV)

Soul Ties

We cannot address strongholds without addressing soul ties. One usually attracts the other. Although this book is not about spiritual warfare, we cannot neglect these aspects.

What Is a Soul Tie?

A soul tie is an emotional bond, or a spiritual connection, that unites one person to another after being intimate with them. It could be through friendship, connection with a family member, sexual intercourse, or a spiritual connection with someone we affectioned dearly. All soul ties are not evil or bad. Let us take, for example, the bond between a husband and wife. A form of soul tie is created when a married couple consumes their marriage through sexual union.

We also have the example of King David from the Bible. David and his friend, Jonathan, had a good soul tie as a result of a close friendship. The Bible tells us in 1 Samuel 18:1(KJV): "And it came to pass, when he had made an end of speaking unto Saul, that the soul of Jonathan was knit with the soul of David, and Jonathan loved him as his own soul."

> "And he said, "'This explains why a man leaves his father and mother and is joined to his wife, and the two are united into one.' Since they are no longer two but one, let no one split apart what God has joined together."
> Matthew 19:5-6 (NLT)

However, I want you to be aware that the opposite can also be true. Bad relationships with the wrong person can also lead us to toxic emotional bonds. As a result, it can cause the people involved in the relationship to have obsessive tendencies, making it hard to end the relationship and move on.

> "Do you not know that he who unites himself with a prostitute is one with her in body? For it is said, "The two will become one flesh."
> I Corinthians 6:16 (NIV)

Signs of a soul tie

- Mood shifts based on the presence, or absence, of the other person.
- Always considering their reaction before making any decision.
- Stalking the other person on social media and unable to stop seeing him/her.

- Staying with the person despite family and friends' protests.
- Willingness to do anything to make the relationship work, despite toxicity.
- Tormented mind.
- Feeling miserable and confused without the other person.
- After many years, still unable to release that person from the mind.
- Unable to leave a toxic environment; always end up going back.
- Wanting to be free but feeling chained.

Though it may be contrary to what you feel, these chains are breakable. Keep in mind that the turning point of your life will depend on what you allow in your mind.

"The chains of habit are too weak to be felt until they are too strong to be broken."
Samuel Johnson

Let us pray!

Heavenly Father, here we are today to surrender our lives to You. Bring light to all the blockages compromising our freedom. We also ask You to break all the toxic connections, fortified reasonings, lies, and distorted ways of thinking that dishonor You. Sanctify our lives. We submit our heart in obedience to Your will. It is in the mighty name of Jesus Christ that we pray.

Amen

Meditation Verses

The Bible tells us:

I Corinthians 6:16 (NIV)

Do you not know that he who unites himself with a prostitute is one with her in body? For it is said, "The two will become one flesh."

1 Samuel 18:1 (ASV)

And it came to pass, when he had made an end of speaking unto Saul, that the soul of Jonathan was knit with the soul of David, and Jonathan loved him as his own soul.

Matthew 19:5 (NIV)

And said, 'For this reason a man will leave his father and mother and be united to his wife, and the two will become one flesh'?

2 Corinthians 10:3-5 (NKJV)

For though we walk in the flesh, we do not war according to the flesh. For the weapons of our warfare are not carnal but mighty in God for pulling down strongholds, casting down arguments and every high thing that exalts itself against the knowledge of God, bringing every thought into captivity to the obedience of Christ.

Philippians 4:8 (NIV)

Finally, brothers and sisters, whatever is true, whatever is noble, whatever is right, whatever is pure, whatever is lovely, whatever is admirable—if anything is excellent or praiseworthy—think about such things.

Romans 12:2 (NIV)

Do not conform to the pattern of this world but be trans-formed by the renewing of your mind. Then you will be able to test and approve what God's will is—his good, pleasing, and perfect will.

Study Questions

1. What are the fears that are holding you back? And what nourishes them?

_____

_____

_____

_____

2. Find three Bible verses that counter the fears you listed in question one.

_____

_____

_____

_____

3. List specific lies you have been believing.

_____

_____

_____

_____

4. Write down three Bible verses that counter those lies.

_____

_____

_____

_____

Notes

Chapter 3

Self-Examination

We must ask ourselves real questions.

As we learned earlier in this book, external events generate thoughts that influence our actions and emotions.

Depending on how we interpret external triggers, positive or negative sentiments are created. As a result, these feelings affect the direction we choose to go.

Once you understand this behavioral cycle, it becomes easier to break free from any negative pattern created by our feelings.

The real stepping stone toward wellness starts within us. It begins in our minds. Again, our lives are not affected by external events, but more by the interpretation given to these events.

"Once we succeed in changing our negative thoughts to positives ones, our actions, behavior and wellness improves."

The techniques we will be discussing center around assessing our thoughts and feelings to determine the difference between facts, emotions, and opinions.

Once we can recognize negative and irrational

perspectives, stop these perspectives, and change them, we can begin to change how we feel and how we behave.

Journaling Through ABCD

Activating event (Situation)

Belief system (Thoughts & Beliefs)

Consequence (Feeling & Behavior)

Dispute (Put your thoughts into the test)

The first technique we will discuss is called **ABCD**. Created by Albert Ellis, Ph.D., this proven, practical approach is used by cognitive therapists during counseling sessions.

This technique consists of four components: the **A**ctivating event, our **B**eliefs, the **C**onsequence, and the **D**ispute. The goal of this approach is to help us break the mind cycle that leads us to self-destruction, irrational thinking, and negativity that consequently causes us to acquire bad habits and behaviors. This self-analysis method is also a tool to address our deep emotions by being aware of our beliefs. Let's begin by defining the four components!

A is the **A**ctivating event, also called the Situation, representing:

- ✧ The initial situation that caused you harm.
- ✧ The trigger.
- ✧ The moment everything started.

B is our Belief system, representing:

✧ What we believe led to the triggering event.

✧ Our understanding and interpretation of the situation.

✧ Our inner conversations.

✧ Where irrational beliefs and lies are created in our heads.

✧ What triggers our emotions.

C is the consequence; it is the outcome of A (the activating event) + B (the Beliefs), representing:

✧ What you think will happen in the short-term and long-term, if you do not change your thinking.

✧ The consequence of your response.

✧ How the event impacts your thoughts, feelings, and behavior.

Simply put, the consequence is the result we get out of the initial situation based on our thoughts, actions, and beliefs.

D is the Dispute, representing:

✧ When we put our thinking to the test.

✧ When we analyze ourselves to see if how we feel makes any sense.

✧ When we try to bring our minds back to a neutral or positive state.

✧ When we examine the beliefs that are causing our unhealthy behaviors.

To give you a better picture of how we can use the **ABCD** assessment method, I implemented an exercise that you will be able to use and recreate every time you go through a hard situation.

Exercise-Inspired by the cognitive ABCD technique

Step 1. Activating event (the situation)

Ask yourself: What happened? According to you, what triggered how you feel?

_____

_____

_____

_____

_____

Step 2. Belief system (thoughts and beliefs)

Ask yourself: What is my understanding of the situation? What do I believe is going on?

_____

_____

_____

_____

_____

Step 3. Consequence (The outcome of B + C)

Ask yourself: How does what happened impact me?

_____

_____

_____

_____

_____

Step 4. Dispute (Put your thoughts to the test)

Ask yourself: Is what I think rational, and based on real facts, or is this the fruit of distorted thoughts?

_____

_____

_____

_____

Step four is the place where you bring your mind back to a neutral, calm state. It can be done through prayer, meditation, breathing exercises, or relaxation techniques.

The other tool that I would like to introduce you to is the mnemonic **PQRSTU**[3] method. This technique is a nursing

---

[3] an interview method of pain assessment.

questioning method used to analyze the degree of pain felt by patients through a verbal interview. It is a matter of questioning the person, who is suffering, to obtain an accurate portrait of the pain they feel and intervene most effectively.

During a tumultuous period of my life, I found therapy from journaling and writing down my feelings. Through documenting, in-depth researching, and questioning, I came to understand myself better—to recognize what was altering my worldview and what was amplifying my emotional discomfort.

Even though this mnemonic device is commonly used for physical pain assessment, emotional pain is still pain. Therefore, you can also use it to assess your emotional distress. Let's look at the version of the **PQRSTU** method I have developed to assess my own emotional pain.

But, just before showing you my redefined version of that golden tool, let's see what the original acronym **PQRSTU** stands for first.

P stands for provocation and palliation.

- ✧ What provokes the pain, and what palliates it?
- ✧ What makes it worse?
- ✧ What makes it better?

Q stands for quality.

- ✧ How do I feel?
- ✧ Is it a burning, cold, or hot, sensation; a sharp, dull, stabbing, prickling sensation, or itching, pinching, and so on?

R stands for region or radiation.

✧ Where is the pain located?
✧ Does the pain move anywhere?
✧ Does it radiate to another place?

S stands for severity

✧ On a scale between 0 to 10, how would you rate the severity of your pain, zero being the lowest level?

T stands for timing.

✧ When did it start?
✧ How often do you feel this way?
✧ Is it constant?
✧ Is it sudden or gradual?
✧ Is it on and off?
✧ Is it only felt at night before you sleep or when you wake up?

U stands for understanding.

✧ What is your understanding of what is going on?

Now that I've explained the **PQRSTU** assessment method, let me introduce you to my version of the assessment, but this time as a tool to assess emotional pain.

As you go through the revised version of the pain assessment questionnaire, I encourage you to take your time to connect the questions to your circumstances and to document them.

This exercise will help you have a more accurate view of your situation and will later help you build your action plan.

Let's get started!

Expounded and redefined **PQRSTU**

🚨 P—**Provocation and Palliation**

Think about what provokes or aggravates your mood or causes pain. It could be any of the following triggers:
- ✧ A thought
- ✧ Someone's presence
- ✧ Words
- ✧ Being alone
- ✧ Returning to specific places
- ✧ Particular objects or possessions
- ✧ A scent, such as perfume
- ✧ A specific song or sound
- ✧ A specific emotional affliction

Now think about what seems to relieve your pain. It could be one or several things from the following list:
- ✧ Listening to music
- ✧ Meditation
- ✧ Prayer
- ✧ Shopping
- ✧ The presence of someone specific
- ✧ Going out with friends

- ✧ Exercising
- ✧ Drinking alcohol
- ✧ Writing
- ✧ Singing
- ✧ Taking drugs
- ✧ Taking sleeping pills
- ✧ Other factors

☹ Q—Qualifying

Write down everything that comes to mind when answering the following questions:

- ✧ How do you feel?
- ✧ What are the emotions you are experiencing?
- ✧ How would you qualify or describe the pain you feel?

R—Region and Radiation

Where do you feel the pain? Where does the discomfort resonate in your body?

A. Is it in one or more of the following forms?

- ✧ An oppression
- ✧ Heaviness or weight on your shoulders
- ✧ Depression
- ✧ Spleen (unexplainable deep pain)
- ✧ A sensation of been paralyzed
- ✧ Shortness of breath

✧ A ball in your throat
✧ An impression that your heart is being ripped out
✧ Other sensations

B. Which region of your body has been affected by your emotional pain?

✧ The heart
✧ The head, brain, or mind
✧ The shoulders (like a dead weight)
✧ The stomach
✧ The kidneys
✧ The lungs
✧ The throat
✧ Other

C. In what area of your life do you feel affected?

✧ Trusting people, by saying: "I am unable to trust again."
✧ Relationships (friendship, partnership, marriage, family, and more)
✧ Physical health
✧ Emotional health
✧ Mental health
✧ Other

"The mind and the body are not separate. What affects one, affects the others."
Unknown

⌒ S—Severity

If you could rate your pain on a scale of 0 to 10, how would you rate it?

Be honest with yourself, and do not compare yourself to others. Once again, pain is relative. Two people can experience the same situation and be affected differently. It is okay for you to feel that your pain is a ten when someone else may experience the same pain and feel that it is only a two. Everyone has a different level of endurance.

⏰ T—Timing

- ✧ When did your pain start?
- ✧ How often do you feel this way?
- ✧ Is it constant?
- ✧ Is it on and off?
- ✧ Is it only felt at night, before you sleep, or when you wake up?
- ✧ When does it seem worse?

For instance, in my personal experience, the mornings and before going to bed were the most difficult times. I could not stop overthinking, and I would sometimes experience intense anxiety. On my strategy plan, I had to implement a morning meditation routine consisting of positive Bible declaration and prayer time before going to bed. I had to continually declare the Word of God over my life to build myself up, either by reading or speaking the Scripture out loud. I cannot thank God enough for a friend who was inspired to put Bible verses into songs for people to remember them easily in times of need.

The constant reminder of God's goodness through songs helped solidify the truths in my heart and mind.

☀ U—Understanding

Understand your situation.

Ask yourself what the root cause of your hardship is, and what is holding you back from being emotionally well. It could be any of the following factors:

- ✧ Spiritual blockage
- ✧ Cognitive distortions
- ✧ Hormone imbalance
- ✧ Other factors

> "For we wrestle not against flesh and blood, but against principalities, against powers, against the rulers of the darkness of this world, against spiritual wickedness in high places."
> Ephesians 6:12 (KJV)

Too many times, we apply the wrong treatment to our symptoms. We attempt to fight physical issues with religious rituals and fight spiritual matters with physical resources. We treat spiritual warfare with medication and try to treat mental illness with religiosity.

Once again, self-analysis must be taken incredibly seriously. Here, the key is to keep on going back to the moment you first started to feel emotionally unwell and, from there, to make an in-depth investigation.

With all the information you have accumulated, you are now ready to complete your analysis and think of an action plan for change.

Keep in mind that the turning point in our lives depends on how we allow our minds to think. Our life changes for the better when we are aware of our mind's thought cycles. As a human being, living on planet Earth, we cannot prevent hardships from coming. We can only change how we think, feel, and react to them.

God never promised us that everything would be easy, nor does He promise us that we will never encounter hardship by having Him in our lives. He promises peace through adversity—a peace that surpasses understanding and transcends our intelligence. And that is what makes the whole difference.

> "And the peace of God, which surpasses all understanding, will guard your hearts and minds through Christ Jesus."
> Philippians 4:7 (NKJV)

As many preachers like to say, there is no expiration date for our deliverance. Keep pushing. You are closer than you think.

The turning points of our lives

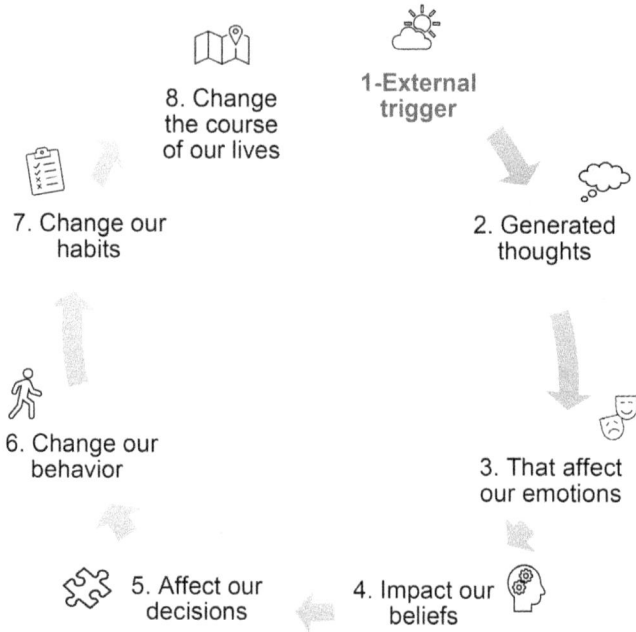

8. Change
the course
of our lives

1-External
trigger

7. Change our
habits

2. Generated
thoughts

6. Change our
behavior

3. That affect
our emotions

5. Affect our
decisions

4. Impact our
beliefs

Let us pray!

Heavenly Father, as we end this chapter, I would like to thank You for Your loving kindness and Your compassion toward us. As You put clarity in our mind, heal our body, mind, and soul from the past. Dethrone everything that took our attention and heart from You. Teach us how to guard our hearts like You are asking us in Proverb 4:23. Take Your place in our hearts, God, and reign again in us. It is in the mighty name of Jesus Christ we pray.
Amen!

Meditation Verses

The Bible tells us:

Psalm 30:11-12 (NKJV)

You have turned for me my mourning into dancing; You have put off my sackcloth and clothed me with gladness, that my heart may sing praise to You and not be silent. O LORD my God, I will give thanks to you forever.

Psalm 30:5 (NLT)

For his anger lasts only a moment, but his favor lasts a lifetime! Weeping may last through the night, but joy comes with the morning.

Psalm 147:3 (NKJV)

He heals the brokenhearted and binds up their wounds.

3 John 1:2 (NKJV)

Beloved, I pray that you may prosper in all things and be in health, just as your soul prospers.

Psalm 23:3 (NKJV)

He restores my soul; He leads me in the paths of righteousness For His name's sake.

Psalm 34:19 (NKJV)

Many are the afflictions of the righteous, But the LORD delivers him out of them all.

Psalm 51:10 (NKJV)

Create in me a clean heart, O God, and renew a steadfast spirit within me.

Romans 8:1-2 (NLT)

So now there is no condemnation for those who belong to Christ Jesus. And because you belong to him, the power of the life-giving Spirit has freed you from the power of sin that leads to death.

Romans 8:28 (NKJV)

And we know that all things work together for good to those who love God, to those who are the called according to His purpose.

Philippians 4:8 (NIV)

Finally, brothers and sisters, whatever is true, whatever is noble, whatever is right, whatever is pure, whatever is lovely, whatever is admirable—if anything is excellent or praiseworthy—think about such things.

Proverb 4:23 (NIV)

Above all else, guard your heart, for everything you do flows from it.

2 Corinthians 10:5 (KJV)

Casting down imaginations, and every high thing that exalteth itself against the knowledge of God and bringing into captivity every thought to the obedience of Christ.

Proverb 23:7 (NKJV)

For as he thinks in his heart, so is he.

Notes

Chapter 4

Learn from the Past, Live in the Present, and Build for Tomorrow

Turn Your Experiences into Lessons Learned.

Have you ever wished you could start your life, or an episode of your existence, over again? Have you ever been haunted by inner paralyzing thoughts? Thoughts such as: *"It should have been…, I would have been…, They should have been…, We should have been…"* If yes, you are not alone. We all have had these thoughts at some point in life. Unfortunately, making peace with the past is not an easy task.

Life is an evolution; time goes by regardless of the decisions we make. Many of us confuse the passing of time with progress. The movement of time carries us into the future without requiring us to do or learn anything. But growth requires us to make efforts, evolve, understand, learn, and achieve something before progress is achieved.

Though it is easier to be carried by time effortlessly, the purpose of life is to fully live God's plan for us, and not to merely survive, or exist, as we watch life pass us by.

> "Do not confuse motion and progress. A rocking horse keeps moving but does not make any progress."
> Alfred A. Montapert

As long as we are still alive, there is hope. With God's help, we can create a better future. With that in mind, it is essential to understand that we must take action. If we want to move forward, we must face any unresolved matters from our past before progress can be made. Again, not to relive the past, but to learn from it and become the person we are called to be.

In every situation, we must reflect on the lessons learned and the understanding gained; forgive ourselves and others, and let go. We must take advantage of our past experiences and use them to create a new ending. We must look through "what was," like we look through a car's rearview mirror—looking ahead and moving forward.

Three questions we can ask ourselves:

1. What can I learn from this situation?
2. Why do I feel like this? What are the emotional patterns my mind has memorized from this?
3. What is my pain trying to tell me?

1. What can I learn from this situation?

First, learning from the past means being aware of the experiences that are affecting us negatively. Then, by figuring out precisely how we have been affected, we come to know what changes need to be made so that we can make positive progress.

To prevent us from repeating the same cycle, we must acknowledge what is wrong with the pattern we want to break.

This allows us to know our weaknesses, readjust our lives, and understand what we want instead of repeating patterns of mistakes and pain.

To improve, we must receive additional knowledge and be willing to put in the work to change. Learning requires a mental effort; it requires us to think, to take the time to write down *what* did not work and *why*. Learning requires us to find new information that will help us build a better conceptual understanding, new neural connections, and make better life choices in the future. We can then apply better judgment and have a more accurate perspective of the things we could not see before.

The ability to be great resides in everyone. Therefore, it is up to each of us to acquire the knowledge we need. Ignorance can no longer be an excuse for failure; it is a self-imposed limitation.

There are lessons to be learned through every hardship in our lives. The hardships we face teach us about ourselves. When we repeatedly face the same struggles, it can be a sign that we are missing an important key of understanding. The best thing to do in that situation is to ask God to reveal the things we do not see and give us a new understanding to do things differently. We cannot expect different results from doing the same things. The same actions will produce the same patterns.

"You are the sum total of all the decisions you made in your life; You are also responsible for who you are today and who you will be tomorrow."

A person who knows better does better. With that in mind, it is always an excellent prayer to ask God to bless us with intelligence, wisdom, and knowledge.

> "For the LORD gives wisdom; from his mouth
> come knowledge and understanding."
> Proverbs 2:6 (NIV)

Solomon was onto something when he asked God for wisdom. Had he asked for riches only, God would have given it to him. However, would he have known how to sustain his wealth without wisdom? Probably not. Wisdom helps us to have sound judgment and learn from our own and other peoples' mistakes; discernment enlightens us with the right perspective for situations that arise in our life.

When necessary, consulting a therapist is great. Yet, this practice should never undermine or cancel the importance of building a relationship with Christ. We need balance. When seeking God's guidance, we can prevent avoidable mistakes. Through prayer, we gain insight into the heart and mind of God, giving us a clear vision of what is coming ahead and helping us to avoid hidden traps.

> "Intelligence is the ability to know what the best thing to do is. Wisdom is the ability to apply that right action."

Proverbs 14:12 and Proverbs 16:25 (NKJV) both tell us, "There is a way that seems right to a man, but its end is the way of death." Only God can save us from some traps.

2. What are the emotional patterns my mind has memorized from this?

The Power of the Mind and Thoughts

Did you know that 60 to 80% of health issues are related to stress or suppressed emotions? Negative emotions and unprocessed life events that are undealt with create emotional patterns that we carry in our minds throughout life. Carrying such baggage from the past does not only cause us to self-sabotage our destiny, but it alters our worldview, causes stress, and makes us physically ill. It puts us at risk of developing all types of chronic disease, creates muscular tension, and leads to unexplained chronic pain. Additionally, the body does not differentiate between a real-life stressful situation and a situation that is fabricated by our thoughts alone. Our bodies are responsive to what we think and feel, and since the mind and the body are connected, what affects one will affect the other.

Did you know that specific emotions affect specific areas of our body, such as the following?

* Fear and fright affect the kidneys, the heart, and bladder, possibly leading to back pain, insomnia, and adrenal fatigue.
* Anger affects the liver, possibly leading to headaches, itching skin, and low energy.
* Worry affects the colon, digestive system, and shoulders.
* Sadness and grief affect the heart and the lungs.

* Stress affects the adrenal glands, the blood vessels, the heart, the digestive system, and possibly leads to insomnia, heart palpitations, muscle cramps, brain fatigue, lack of concentration, and more.
* Anxiety affects the lungs, the large intestine, and more.

> "The circumstances that surround a man's life are not important. How that man responds to those circumstances is what's important. His response is the ultimate determining factor between success and failure."
> Booker T. Washington

I will never stress enough that everything begins in our minds. In fact, thinking is the function of the mind that figures things out. It gives meaning to every single life event. It creates a concept and the ideas through which we define a situation, relationships, problems, and feelings.

Dr. Patrick Gentempo once said: "What you thought before has led to every choice you made, and this adds up to you at this moment. Therefore, if you want to change who you are physically, mentally, and spiritually, you will have to change what you think."

Our current life situation is a direct result of our thoughts and past decisions. What we are inside transposes to our reality through

> "The wrong perspectives will make you hold on to the wrong people, wrong mindset and the wrong things."

feelings and actions. Once we understand what influences our thinking and behavior, we can change it; as a result, we change our destination.

Now, what is it that influences our thoughts?

The primary factor that influences our thinking is our neural connections, acquired through experiences. When coming across a situation, our thoughts regroup ideas, consult memorized emotions from similar events from our past, and come to an understanding.

Based on the concepts built by our neural association and our comprehension of an event, emotional reactions and body responses are created.

Our mindset is vital; we become, and we attract what we think or believe.

> "For the thing I greatly feared has come upon me, and what I dreaded has happened to me."
> Job 3:25 (NKJV)

We become the sum of our thoughts, decisions, and actions. And our thoughts determine whether what we are considering is good or bad. Staying too long in the same negative mindset alters the lenses through which we analyze our overall life events, and this altered mindset eventually affects our beliefs. Therefore, we need to bring to light all the recorded sentiments that have altered our way of thinking and replace them with the right mindset.

We also have to forgive ourselves for anything that causes us to live in continuous guilt. We should not have to live in constant regret for not meeting our own expectations, or after making a wrong decision. We must change our mindset to have a Christ-like mentality and believe that God can change our circumstances for the better.

3. What is my pain communicating to me?

Emotional Memory and the Benefits of Pain

Learning from the past involves open-mindedness about the feelings we are experiencing. Our feelings represent signals that warn us when something needs to be taken care of immediately.

I once watched a documentary on the sense of pain. It was the story of a five-year-old girl who could not feel pain due to a pathological condition. Consequently, her parents had to constantly keep her under surveillance to make sure she would not hurt herself. Unfortunately, one day, the little girl injured herself so severely that she lost vision in one eye. Without the ability to feel pain, she had no idea of the extent to which she could injure herself.

Pain is a teacher that records a sense of danger in our minds. It is an indicator that something is wrong. It helps us establish boundaries and not repeat the same mistakes that lead us to hurt. It can be a physical or an emotional sensation, but both function the same way. Emotional distress makes us aware that there is something that requires our attention.

"A man must be big enough to admit his mistakes, smart enough to profit from them, and strong enough to correct them." John C. Maxwell

Sadly, since emotional pain is not always tangible, many people choose to mute the discomfort intentionally or unconsciously by minimizing or masking it with distractions, such as self-medication, alcohol, self-mutilation, drugs, indifference, introversion, isolation, overeating, not eating, or anything else that can help them escape reality.

The danger of muting our feelings is that we cannot select the emotions that we numb. By trying to control our negative sentiments, we also develop coping mechanisms that dull all our emotions. For instance, by denying sadness, hurt, or other negative emotions, we also limit ourselves from experiencing real joy, freedom, and happiness, and we end up living disconnected from reality. Not to mention that muting the pain without facing the real problem behind it only makes the issues worse.

Suppressing our emotions does not stop the pain from damaging us, nor does it show we are stronger than others. It is an indication that our minds are in survival mode and are developing protective mechanisms that strive to separate us from reality.

We can summarize that the goal should never be to avoid unpleasant emotions but rather to examine these emotions, understand them, learn from them, and let them go.

We must process our feelings, not suppress them. Emotions allow us to understand ourselves and others, and to be understood by others. They serve us as red flags, showing us what we think. They also show us where there may be remaining wounds in specific areas of our lives.

Pain is part of a healthy life balance. It is a sign that we are still alive, and it develops a problem-solving mindset in us.

The focus is to acquire tools that help us break the negative patterns quicker and to use these warning signs to act. We can also make a keen examination of ourselves by studying our emotions. They say a stitch in time saves nine. I would say: paying attention to the warning signs will lead to healing faster.

Let us pray!

Dear God, what are the mesmerizing emotions that are altering my character? What are the things that I need to learn from my past? What is it that my pain is communicating to me? Father, give me clarity, knowledge, discernment, understanding, and wisdom. Renew my mind and give me a new way of thinking. It is in the mighty name of Jesus Christ I pray.
Amen

Keep Asking, Seeking, Knocking!

Meditation Verses

The Bible tells us:

James 1:5 (NIV)

If any of you lacks wisdom, he should ask God, who gives generously to all without finding fault, and it will be given to you.

Proverbs 10:13 (NKJV)

Wisdom is found on the lips of him who has understanding, but a rod is for the back of him who is devoid of understanding.

Proverbs 16:16 (NIV)

How much better to get wisdom than gold, to get insight rather than silver!

Matthew 7: 7-8 (NKJV)

Ask, and it will be given to you; seek, and you will find; knock, and it will be opened to you. For everyone who asks receives; and he who seeks finds, and to him who knocks it will be opened.

2 Corinthians 1:4-6 (NIV)

Who comforts us in all our troubles, so that we can comfort those in any trouble with the comfort we ourselves receive from God. For just as we share abundantly in the sufferings of Christ, so also our comfort abounds through Christ. If we are distressed, it is for your comfort and salvation; if we are comforted, it is for your comfort, which produces in you patient endurance of the same sufferings we suffer.

Romans 15:4 (NKJV)

For whatever things were written before were written for our learning, that we through the patience and comfort of the Scriptures might have hope.

2 Corinthians 4:17-18 (NIV)

For our light and momentary troubles are achieving for us an eternal glory that far outweighs them all. So we fix our eyes not on what is seen, but on what is unseen, since what is seen is temporary, but what is unseen is eternal.

Proverbs 16:25 (NKJV)

There is a way that seems right to a man, but its end is the way of death.

Proverbs 14:12-13 (NKJV)

There is a way that seems right to a man, But its end is the way of death. Even in laughter the heart may sorrow, and the end of mirth may be grief.

Study Questions

1. What have my past mistakes taught me?

_____

_____

_____

2. Knowing what I know today, what can I do differently?

_____

_____

_____

3. Knowing what I know now, what advice would I give to my former self?

_____

_____

_____

4. What is the importance of seeking the intelligence and wisdom of God?

_____

_____

_____

5. What are the benefits of praying for discernment?

_____

_____

_____

Notes

_____

_____

_____

_____

_____

_____

_____

_____

_____

_____

_____

_____

_____

_____

_____

_____

Learn from the Past, Live in the Present, and Build for Tomorrow

_____

_____

_____

_____

_____

_____

_____

_____

_____

_____

Chapter 5

We Must Fill Our Cup with the Right Things

Be Set Free!

"Worry does not empty tomorrow of its sorrow. It empties today of its strength." -Corrie Ten Boom

> "Finally, brothers and sisters, whatever is true, whatever is noble, whatever is right, whatever is pure, whatever is lovely, whatever is admirable—if anything is excellent or praiseworthy—think about such things."
> Philippians 4:8 (NIV)

After reflecting on our past, we are now ready to build our wellness action plan. Again, to be well, we must be filled with the right mentality. The correct mindset demands that we empty our mind of all false beliefs that we may have accumulated and fill it with the proper perspective.

To make it easier to identify the elements we want to discard, the first thing we must do is establish our definition of wellness. Once we do, our next step will be to identify where we are situated in our healing process; and, based on our answer, set up clear goals for the change we would like to see or where we would like to be in the future. We need a plan with clear directions.

Taking Action

Earlier in the book, we saw the importance of being honest with ourselves, acknowledging how we feel, documenting our journey, and learning from our experiences. Although these steps are vital to our healing, we must understand that they are not enough to bring complete recovery.

To see fundamental changes in our lives, we must take real action with all the information that we have gathered. Our willingness to be free or having good intentions is a great start, but it is not enough.

Have you ever heard the saying, "The road to hell is paved with good intentions?" Intentions do not get us where we want to be. It is, perhaps, an excellent starting point, but it is the actions that follow our plan that will determine where we end up, which is what this action plan is all about.

An action plan is a proposed method of strategy that contains our intentions with the actions we plan to execute to reach our objective.

> "Effort and courage are not enough without purpose and direction."
> John F. Kennedy

The benefit of having a guideline is that it helps us to have a visual point of reference regarding what we are working toward. It helps us evolve and have a clearer vision of what we are trying to achieve rather than just going with the flow.

Contrary to the common belief that "time heals all wounds", time alone does not heal anything. We need to act. It takes courage to change. Change requires us to make decisions, to be determined, to analyze ourselves, to research, to ask questions, to seek knowledge, to pray, and to meditate. These things cultivate the right mentality.

As you go through the following sections of the book, let me encourage you not to give up! There is a lot of information to assimilate, and if you are like most people, you may feel the desire to see changes happen instantly.

We must take it one day at a time and be patient with ourselves. We cannot make it on our own strength. God is the one who perfects us. While He is the one operating healing in us, it does not take away our responsibility to work on ourselves. It simply allows us to partner with Him.

God and Our Wellness Journey

To survive amid adversity, we need to fix our eyes on the right things. The more we focus on what makes us sad, the more sentiments of sadness will be reinforced.

The Bible tells us in Isaiah 26:3 (ESV): "You keep him in perfect peace, whose mind is stayed on You, because he trusts in you." (Emphasis *mind*.)

> "God may lead us through narrow ways, but He will never lead us astray."

That is why our focus needs to be on God and putting our trust entirely in Him. We cannot talk about wellness without acknowledging God. He is the One who created us and knows what we are made of. He is the One who can give us perfect peace.

When our car has an issue, we bring it back to its manufacturer. When our phone has a problem, we send it back to the provider. The same should apply to us. When we experience difficulties, we must develop a reflex of consulting our Maker, our Heavenly Father, and trusting Him with our lives.

God wants to see us well more than we want it for ourselves. He knows what we are made of. Consequently, He knows precisely what we need and what is best for us. That is why we need to trust Him and let Him have His way in our lives to succeed on this journey. He is the only One who knows how many days we have left to live, and in His sovereignty, He has set things in order according to His divine, perfect plan.

Truth be told, we will not always understand the will of God for our lives, and sometimes, His decisions will seem unfair. However, that is where faith comes into play.

God always knows the best thing to do.

Once again, our journey toward wellness is a step-by-step process. We must acknowledge that God is the one who has the final say. He is the one driving the train, and He has the map in His hands.

> "Your word is a lamp to my feet
> and a light to my path."
> Psalm 119:105 (NKJV)

We find our way, our identity, and our purpose by holding on to God's Word, seeking, searching, and getting to know who He is.

What is Faith?
Faith is the ability to trust without seeing.
Faith is what moves the heart of God, not our
tears neither our fears.
Faith is having complete hope, trust, and
confidence in someone or something.
Faith is a conviction, an expectation, an
assurance.
Faith is what moves God.
Faith is what we need to heal.

The Presence of God Makes the Journey Complete

Nowadays, we hear about positive thinking everywhere. There are positive quotes, motivational speakers, daily positive declarations, chakra realignment, and many other things to refresh our mindset or boost our ego. Thinking positive is great, and it is known to positively impact our physical and mental health. Still, it is essential to understand that a motivational speech will not be enough to sustain us throughout the journey of life. If positive thinking brings us 50% of the way on our journey, it is the presence of God that completes the mission. Nothing can replace the emptiness we have in our hearts, because is meant to be filled by God alone. It is the Holy Spirit that helps us finish the race.

What Jesus speaks of in Matthew 12 has been majorly overlooked by our generation.

"When an evil spirit leaves a person, it goes into the desert, seeking rest but finding none. Then it says, I will return to the person I came from. So, it returns and finds its former home empty, swept, and in order. Then the spirit finds seven other spirits eviler than itself, and they all enter the person and live there. And so that person is worse off than before. That will be the experience of this evil generation."
—*Matthew 12:43-45 (NLT)*

In this chapter, Jesus shares how, when evil spirits are cast out of a person, they are sent to the wilderness but come back later to check out the place they left. If the site is found empty, swept, and in order, the spirit does not only resettle there but shows up with seven spirits more evil than itself, making the person's condition worse than before.

Many people wonder why they, after repeatedly praying for the same situations, still feel unable to be free, or keep going back to the same things they were once delivered from. We can learn from Matthew 12 that one of the reasons the evil spirit was able to resettle in the same place is because it remained empty. The problem with remaining empty of the presence of God is that the place stays available for whatever, or whoever, wants to come in. This is how the things we once eliminated come back, and usually, they come back stronger than they were before.

People often keep their old habits, sadness, depression, or the same state of mind because of the remaining void within them. Unfortunately, this is how cycles are created. This becomes one of the main factors that cause believers to lose hope for their situation and to be left wondering if they were ever delivered. That is why many people walk in circles, are confused, lost, and clueless, thinking they are moving forward, while, in fact, they went nowhere but back to their starting point. It is one thing to cast out negative thoughts or spirits from our lives, but what do we fuel ourselves with afterward? That is what makes the difference.

Jesus is the Truth We Need to Remain Free

Scripture is crystal clear on the fact that whoever the Son sets free is free indeed (John 8:36). To be, or remain, free, the Word of God, which is the truth, needs to dwell in our hearts and minds. We need to know God, and we need an encounter with the Holy Spirit, the great Comforter that our Father gave us.

Jesus said, "If you hold to my teaching, you are really my disciples. Then you will know the truth, and the truth will set you free."
—John 8:31-32 (NIV)

Jesus answered, "I am the way and the truth and the life. No one comes to the Father except through me. If you really know me, you will know my Father as well. From now on, you do know him and have seen him."
—John 14:6-7 (NIV)

"If you love me, keep my commands. And I will ask the Father, and he will give you another advocate to help you and be with you forever— the Spirit of truth. The world cannot accept him because it neither sees him nor knows him. But you know him, for he lives with you and will be in you."
—John 14: 15-17 (NIV)

As Christians, we cannot afford to be aloof. We must be aware of the evil one and his schemes, as 2 Corinthians 2:11 advises. One of the tools often used by the devil is ignorance. Ignorance can no longer be an excuse. We have everything it takes to be free.

The knowledge of truth brings down the walls of ignorance; it brings deliverance; it gives peace and allows us to exceed our limitations by expanding our minds.

Keep Your Truth Reservoir Full

It is essential to keep our "truth reservoir" full of God. Who likes to drive a car on empty? Keeping yourself full of God will be your safety net.

When we are full of the words of power, peace, love, liberty, faith, and hope that God provides, it allows us to believe in His big plan. We impact our surroundings as this truth overflows from us.

It is hard to feel depressed, sad, down, and stressed out when our eyes are fixed on God. We begin to worry and live in fear when we allow such things into our lives: losing focus, losing hope by not believing in a better tomorrow, doubting His Word that promises He cares for us, feeling overwhelmed, comparing ourselves to others, focusing on what we are missing, or on what others think of us.

If I could summarize this chapter into one single truth, it would be to seek the kingdom of God first, and everything else will follow.

By repositioning ourselves to move toward the right goals, to have the right mentality and the right priorities, and to focus on the kingdom of heaven, everything else will follow, and all our needs will be met.

We cannot go wrong when we choose to make God the center of our lives. While we seek Him, we find peace, joy, provision, purpose, identity, and freedom.

Wellness is the excellent health and harmony of your mind, your body, your spirit, and your soul. Remember that God, who created us, wants us to be well more than we want it for ourselves.

It is now time to add a section to our action plan, dedicated on ways to be filled by the Holy Spirit. For example, it can be done by implementing a meditation schedule, or a Bible reading time, prayer time, and more. To develop the right mind frame and eliminate the things that hold us back, our mind needs to be restored. The goal is to be found full of our loving God, the Truth. The principle behind is to empty and to be refilled by the right things. After emptying ourselves, we must find good replacements to fill the voids. This makes an explosive combination in our wellness journey. Restore: To put back into order or use. "Time can't make something grow that doesn't exist; to be healed, we must cultivate the right mentality."

Let us pray!

*Father, thank You for Your provision and unconditional love. Thank
You for Your kindness, compassion, grace, and mercy. Lord, I pray that
You would impact our mind, body, and soul at this moment.
Let Your presence give us hope, and may our spirit and soul be
encouraged at this moment.
Remove from our mind all the wrong beliefs, judgment, knowledge,
sickness, or anything that is holding us back from being well in the
mighty name of Jesus Christ.
Enlighten our mind, spirit, and soul; help
us see clearly, like never before.
It is in the mighty name of Jesus Christ I pray.
Amen*

Meditation Verses

The Bible tells us:

Ephesians 3:19 (ESV)

And to know the love of Christ that surpasses knowledge, that
you may be filled with all the fullness of God.

Psalm 103:5 (NLT)

He fills my life with good things. My youth is renewed like the
eagle's!

Psalm 107:6-9 (NLT)

LORD, help!" they cried in their trouble, and he rescued them from their distress. He led them straight to safety, to a city where they could live. Let them praise the LORD for his great love and for the wonderful things he has done for them. For he satisfies the thirsty and fills the hungry with good things.

Romans 5:3-5 (NLT)

We can rejoice, too, when we run into problems and trials, for we know that they help us develop endurance. And endurance develops strength of character, and character strengthens our confident hope of salvation. And this hope will not lead to disappointment. For we know how dearly God loves us, because he has given us the Holy Spirit to fill our hearts with his love.

Romans 15:13 (NLT)

I pray that God, the source of hope, will fill you completely with joy and peace because you trust in him. Then you will overflow with confident hope through the power of the Holy Spirit.

Study Questions

1. What is your definition of wellness?

_____

_____

_____

_____

2. Where do you stand on your wellness journey?

_____

_____

_____

_____

3. What are your wellness goals?

_____

_____

_____

_____

4. What are the things you need to improve on your journey?

_____

_____

_____

_____

5. What strategies can you implement to be filled with the Word of God?

_____

_____

_____

_____

6. What is the self-talk, habit, or thing that you want to get rid of?

_____

_____

_____

_____

7. Why is it not good to remain empty?

_____

_____

_____

_____

Notes

_____

_____

_____

_____

_____

_____

_____

_____

_____

_____

_____

_____

_____

_____

_____

_____

_____

_____

_____

_____

_____

_____

Chapter 6

Rebuilding Your Self-Esteem and God-Confidence

Understanding your identity.

We Are Children of the Most High God.

> "Keep your heart with all diligence,
> For out of it spring the issues of life."
> Proverbs 4:23 (NKJV)

There are many means by which we can build our self-esteem. The purpose of this chapter is to seek to provide you with these means. It is all about learning how to reclaim your authority and applying practical keys that will help us find healing, peace, inner growth, and purpose.

Like we saw in the previous chapter, we must empty our lives from all the toxic things we have accumulated and subsequently fill ourselves with the right things.

Garbage in, garbage out (GIGO) is not just a cliché but a fact. Invented by George Fuechsel, an IBM teacher and programmer, this sentence was used to remind his students that a computer only processes what it has been programmed with. A bad input generates a bad output. We must be always extremely vigilant with the things we introduce into our lives, such as what we watch, read, listen to, and even our environments and circle of friends.

> "Above all else, guard your heart, for everything you do flows from it. Keep your mouth free of perversity; keep corrupt talk far from your lips. Let your eyes look straight ahead; fix your gaze directly before you. Give careful thought to the[c] paths for your feet and be steadfast in all your ways. Do not turn to the right or the left; keep your foot from evil."
> Proverb 4: 23-27 (NIV)

Self-esteem is someone's confidence in their ability and worth. The same way faith comes from what we hear, our beliefs come from what we allow inside our minds.

The first thing we must do to gain confidence is to put down our masks and be authentic.

Often, we wear masks because we fear rejection. We present ourselves to others the way we think they would like us. Then we develop strategies to camouflage who we truly are and how we feel. In this chapter, I want to help you realize that it is okay to be yourself. It is now time to put the masks down and be free.

In life, we must make peace with the fact that:

We will not be appealing to everyone.
We will not be accepted by everyone.
We will not be understood by everyone.
We will not be loved by everyone.
We will not be approved by everyone.
We will not be appreciated by everyone.
We will not be acknowledged by everyone.
We will not be forgiven by everyone.
And we will be judged based on past mistakes.

From there, the only thing we can do, and the only thing we are in control of, is to love others, follow Christ, be ourselves, be kind to others, and move forward! Most of the time, people who judge us do not even know us. They pass judgment based on the representation of us that they have in their mind. Yet again, they do not know us. We live in an era where people specialize in character assassination, in the name of "holy discernment" or "holy judgment."

That is why it is essential to know ourselves and not let the judgment of people tell us who we are. Their judgment cannot determine where we are going, our ability to change, or our purpose. If there is breath in your lungs, every day is a new opportunity for you to get better, be better, know better, and do better. As long as we live, nothing is final.

Detoxify Your Mind

It is vital to cultivate the right mindset for our well-being. Like we have seen in previous chapters, feeding ourselves with

God's truth is important. Spending time in God's Word allows us to find peace and stability in His presence, and to be influenced by the Holy Spirit.

The Bible tells us in Romans 12:2 not to conform ourselves to this world but to seek to be transformed by the renewing of our minds.

When we immerse ourselves in the Word of God, our perspectives change, and we begin to love ourselves as we ought to.

We Must Try New Things

To generate substantial change in our lives, let us be willing to do things in a way we never have before. This will allow us to discover talents we never knew we had and help us make new decisions that we never thought possible.

Pride Versus Confidence; Humility Versus Low Self-Esteem

It has been a long-standing myth in the Church that, to be humble, we must appear lowly and allow others to walk all over us. Subsequently, some Christians have suffered abuse as part of what they believed was "God's will to live a Christian life."

This lie must be buried today. God wants us to see ourselves the way He sees us. He wants us to see ourselves from His perspective. Low self-esteem is not humility; on the other hand, God does not call us to be prideful. We need balance and knowing our self-worth will help us in achieving that balance. Seeing ourselves as God sees us will allow us to refuse to believe the lies that tell us we are not enough, as well as the lies leading us to believe that we are above everybody else.

> "For I say, through the grace given unto me, to every man that is among you, not to think of himself more highly than he ought to think; but to think soberly, according as God hath dealt to every man the measure of faith."
> Romans 12:3 (KJV)

Making Jesus the center of our lives:

Making Jesus the center of our lives is the most important step in gaining confidence. Contrary to popular beliefs, the most efficient way to gain self-esteem is not to focus on ourselves, but to get to know our Creator, in whom we can discover our identity.

We live in a time when we are encouraged to be selfish, self-centered, self-sufficient, lovers of money, lovers of fame, and everything else that brings us self-gratification. We need to stop making everything about ourselves and put God back at the center of our lives.

By getting to know our Creator, we see our reflection in Him. Getting to know Him is the best way to get to know ourselves on a deeper level. We are created in the image of God, not to be worshiped but to rule and reign over the earth.

The Bible tells us in Philippians 4:13 that we can do all things through Christ, who strengthens us. Now, if self-esteem is defined as confidence in our ability and our worth, and the Bible tells us that we can do all things through Christ, then the more we get to know who Christ is, the more we increase our faith in what we can achieve through God.

Knowing who God is helps us to reposition ourselves toward the right goals and the right priority. Having the wrong priorities keeps us focused on the wrong things, preventing us from reaching our calling. When we align our priorities to God's divine order, then seeking the "Kingdom first, and all its benefits" is no longer a simple verse or a slogan; it becomes our reality.

By making Christ our priority, our focus is no longer on the things that will harm us but rather, on the Healer. He takes care of our mental, emotional, spiritual, physical, and financial well-being. Through this, we get to know the heart of God.

When we see ourselves as God sees us, and know our God-given identity, it is hard not to be confident. For example, let us think about Paul, who was bitten by a snake, and rather than being scared, he shook it off into the fire. Paul was so confident in whom he was serving, and in his own identity, that he was unfazed by the snake and remained focused on his mission. He knew the God whom he served and firmly believed that no snake could remove him from his mission. His reservoir of faith was full!

Another example from Paul's experience is when he was put in jail. While he was captive, he wrote letters to encourage the Church. With his mission in mind, he did not think for a moment that his imprisonment had ended his ministry. Putting Paul in jail could not stop him.

How Does God See Me?

This is the question we should base our perspectives on. Keep in mind that, when we see ourselves as God does, it becomes tough for us to settle for less.

A useful exercise that you can add to your action plan is to make visuals of biblical promises and hang them in your home. These will serve as reminders of God's faithfulness. You will be amazed to see how well this works.

What I find interesting is that you can always readjust your vision while evaluating it over time. Throughout our intentional, conscious pursuit of God, we are blessed to have the Word of God in which we find every solution. The Bible is where we find the methods to break the vicious mindsets that arise to disturb our peace.

May the Spirit of God help you understand you are not the trauma you have experienced in your past. May the Lord grant you a new sense of boldness, love, wisdom, and courage to not give up. May your faith develop exponentially, and may you have a higher hope in Jesus Christ. Moreover, may your spirit understand that God is greater than your current circumstances.

> Seeking the Kingdom first means: To place God above all things; To make it a priority to get to know God; To make it a priority to understand how the kingdom of God functions; To make our Father's business our priority.

Let Us Pray!

Father God, we surrender our hearts to You. May Your Holy Spirit detoxify us to the core. Help us see ourselves the way You see us; neither more nor less. Readjust our spiritual lenses to see things the way You do. Give us the strength to cut all the cords that are connecting us to toxicity. Forgive us for every form of pride and all our shortcomings. It is in the mighty name of Jesus Christ I pray.
Amen

Meditation Verses

The Bible tells us:

Philippians 4:13 (NKJV)

I can do all things through Christ who strengthens me.

Psalm 139:13-14 (NIV)

For you created my inmost being; you knit me together in my mother's womb. I praise you because I am fearfully and wonderfully made; your works are wonderful, I know that full well.

2 Timothy 1:7 (NKJV)

For God has not given us a spirit of fear, but of power and of love and of a sound mind.

Joshua 1:9 (NIV)

Have I not commanded you? Be strong and courageous. Do not be afraid; do not be discouraged, for the LORD your God will be with you wherever you go.

2 Corinthians 12:9 (NKJV)

And He said to me, "My grace is sufficient for you, for My strength is made perfect in weakness." Therefore, most gladly I will rather boast in my infirmities, that the power of Christ may rest upon me.

Proverbs 14:26 (NKJV)

In the fear of the LORD there is strong confidence, And His children will have a place of refuge.

Isaiah 43:4 (NIV)

Since you are precious and honored in my sight, and because I love you, I will give people in exchange for you, nations in exchange for your life.

Hebrews 13:6 (NIV)

So we say with confidence, "The Lord is my helper; I will not be afraid. What can mere mortals do to me?"

Ephesians 2:10 (NLT)

For we are God's masterpiece. He has created us anew in Christ Jesus, so we can do the good things he planned for us long ago.

Mark 9:23 (NKJV)

Jesus said to him, "If you can believe, all things are possible to him who believes."

Study Questions

1. What does the Bible say about you?

_____

_____

_____

_____

2. What are the things you can do to have the right mindset and see yourself the way God sees you?

_____

_____

_____

_____

Notes

_____

_____

_____

_____

_____

_____

_____

_____

_____

_____

_____

_____

_____

_____

_____

_____

_____

_____

_____

_____

_____

_____

_____

_____

_____

_____

_____

_____

_____

Chapter 7

Finding Balance

Body-mind-soul-spirit.

Letting go symbolizes both an end and a new beginning.

> "Beloved, I pray that you may prosper in all
> things and be in health, just as your soul
> prospers."
> 3 John 1:2 (NKJV)

Throughout this book, we have seen many factors that can make us feel like we will never be able to let go. This can be due to an injustice or a broken heart, or it could be strongholds created by a soul tie or long-standing lies that infiltrated our beliefs, or any other factor. One thing all these circumstances have in common is that they are breakable.

It is normal to be afraid to face pain, but this is a perception that makes you *feel* like you cannot be free. It is our perspective that makes us think it will hurt too much to let go. Now, It is up to us to restructure our viewpoint, in accordance with the Bible, and build an action plan to find healing and wellness.

The four stages of healing are:

1. Denial
2. Anger, frustration, or confusion
3. Sadness, grief, or depression
4. Acceptance and steps toward healing

In what phase of healing do you find yourself in right now?

Healing is the acceptance of what was. It is the attainment of peace in the present, where pain has been transformed into scars and becomes a memory.

We cannot erase what we have experienced and expect things to go back to the way they were before. But we can create a better future with the lessons learned through the experience.

Wellness is a state of complete well-being. It is the excellent health of the mind, body, spirit, and soul. We must take care of each of these parts of our being to create a healthy balance. With that in mind, we cannot talk about wellness without acknowledging God and spirituality. Often, the invisible and spiritual part of our being is neglected; this is one way our lives can become imbalanced.

As previously stated, what we go through on a spiritual and emotional level also affects us physically. When it is not properly dealt with, we can develop diseases in our body, such as cancer, diabetes, high blood pressure, heart attacks, kidney failure, and more.

> "Our external world reflects our inner world. To change the outer, we must first change from the inside."

The key to a successful holistic balance is to be mindful of our entire being.

The mind is the central connection point where we can explore how we are doing at the very core of our being. Our mind is controlled by our thoughts. Our thoughts play the role of a steering wheel by giving directives to the mind; it is where dreams, emotions, stress, decisions, actions, and more are born.

Did you know that our mind can only hold one thought at a time? Therefore, to eliminate the negativity in our minds, we must replace it with something. Again, the goal is not to avoid feeling negative emotions but rather to not dwell on them.

In the following paragraphs, you will find separate sections filled with easy and concrete tips that you can implement into your action plan.

Let's get started!

Use Breathing and Meditation to Your Advantage

Breathing is essential to our general health and well-being. Did you know that the way we breathe affects our whole body? Have you ever noticed how you breathe when experiencing stress versus how you breathe when you are in a relaxed, calm mood?

When we experience stress, our brain sends signals and adrenaline to our body, enlarging our lungs, increasing our breathing rate, heart rate, and blood pressure to get ready for any dangerous situation. On the other side, intentional deep breathing sends a message to our brain to calm down and relax. Focusing on your breath in times of stress has been proven to reduce anxiety. Breathing exercises and meditation are the bomb!

Meditation enhances our self-awareness and promotes emotional health. It also generates a better control of anxiety and plays on your mood. Deep breathing exercises are easy to do and can be done anywhere. Next time you find yourself in a tense situation, I encourage you to try.

Meditation on the Word of God while practicing deep breathing once per day is known to reduce our stress in a significant way. Meditating on Bible verses cultivates in us the fruit of the Spirit. If we look closely at the fruit of the Spirit, it is a result of a healthy, balanced relationship with God that generates patience, love, peace, joy, and more. And that is exactly what we want!

As a daily meditation practice for myself, I replace every negative, toxic thought with seven positive biblical statements. I write them down where I can keep them as a visual and meditate on them.

Use Food to Your Advantage: Eat and Drink the Right Things

There is a strong correlation between our mental and emotional health and nutrition. The same way our lungs and blood need oxygen to keep us healthy, we need nourishment for our bodies. What we eat plays a significant role in our energy and wellness.

Did you know that a poor diet could not only affect you physically, but it can affect your mood, too? For example, lemon water, greens, vegetables, nuts, and seeds are known to boost the body's energy. Water is a must if we want to keep ourselves hydrated. Like oxygen and nutrition, water is crucial for our well-being. Did you know that the average human adult body is made up of 50 to 65% water? There are different opinions on how much water we should drink per day, but the general amount recommended by doctors is approximately two liters, or eight glasses, of water per day.

For more information, I recommend you find a good dietitian to discuss proper diet plan options.

Use Exercise to Your Advantage: Move and Stay Active

Staying active will exponentially increase your level of wellness. It is also known to improve our level of concentration and decrease our stress levels. Exercise will help you maintain a great mental balance. Another positive point about physical activity is that it helps us keep a correct posture and removes unnecessary muscle stress. Beyond that, having a good posture helps with self-confidence.

If you suffer from injuries, I encourage you to consult a physical coach with whom you will be able to establish measurable goals.

If you are living on a budget, the good news is that there are many free activities you can do, such as hiking, exercising in nature, online exercise videos, jogging, swimming, and more. Be creative! Ten minutes of daily exercise can help you exponentially! My friend, we must be intentional on our well-being journey. Every single step counts.

Use Your Sleep to Your Advantage: Healthy Sleep Routines

Sleep plays a vital role in our general health. It provides us with significant mental and physical benefits. It is during our sleep that our body is recovering and healing itself. Furthermore, a miserable night of sleep increases our level of stress and, in the long term, can increase the risk of stroke and heart disease. Not to mention we get more impatient and have a bad mood when tired.

As we chase our goals, let us take the time to rest. Here are some recommendations that can help you have better nights:

1. Avoid large meals before bedtime.
2. Avoid caffeine before bedtime.
3. Create a quiet, dark atmosphere with a comfortable temperature.
4. One hour before bedtime, log out of all social media, and put away any electronic device that could disturb your sleep.

Getting a good night of sleep will improve your mood, performance, and concentration.

It can be challenging at first but, gradually, you will get there. Keep in mind that the average person needs about eight hours of sleep each night. However, go with what works best for you, and what your doctor recommends.

Use Your Appearance to Your Advantage: Keep Yourself Clean and Well-groomed

Work with what you have. Your body is the temple of God. He made you the way you are for a reason; learn how to take care of it! How we feel about ourselves affects us in so many ways.

To be well balanced, learn to do things that enhance your looks and makes you feel comfortable in your skin.

For example:

> ➤ Learn about your physical shape and select suitable clothes that will make you feel great about your appearance, bringing glory to God.
>
> ➤ Learn beauty tips that will allow you to feel comfortable and confident.
>
> ➤ Go to the spa and pamper yourself. If you live on a tight budget, you can treat yourself in the comfort of your own home with inexpensive products and a nice, warm bath.
>
> ➤ Build a hygiene routine that will help you feel refreshed and confident.

Create a Positive Environment

Many things can influence our mood and create a positive atmosphere around us. Consider the following ideas to help you improve your daily environment:

* Set the lighting of your house in a way you enjoy.
* Play praise and worship music in the background to create the desired atmosphere.
* Decorate your house the way you know will make you feel peaceful.
* Hang scripture notes and verses around your house to remind you of your worth in God.
* Burn candles that create a pleasant scent in your house.
* If you like to read, get some good new books.

Have you ever watched the movie *War Room?* Have you noticed the way the prayer room was decorated? If not, I recommend it to you as a source of inspiration.

Once again, be creative. Set the atmosphere in a way that will bring you peace.

Communicate with Others and Express Emotions, Needs, Fears, and Opinions

God created us for community. What this means is that God, the Creator of the universe, created us as social beings. Relationships are vital. Everyone needs someone to talk to.

Friendship is known to have a significant impact on health and well-being. Experiencing secure social connections is vital to maintaining a healthy lifestyle. When you have healthy social interactions, it helps you cope with stressful situations. If you are more on the introverted side and struggle to build lasting relationships, I pray that God helps you in that sphere. Trust Him. He will amaze you!

Celebrate Your Small Victories and Find Reasons to be Grateful

"A grateful heart is a magnet for miracles."
Unknown

Set daily goals, and when you achieve them, celebrate your small victories. Focusing on small, achievable goals instead of long-term goals will build a more positive mindset that will help you not feel overwhelmed or lose sight of your end goal.

Discover Yourself and Your God-given Talents

Get to know yourself. Discover new passions, things that entertain you, and that you enjoy doing. Get out of your comfort zone and educate yourself.

* Learn and discover new things.
* Engage in various forms of recreational activities you find interesting.
* Be open-minded to try new food or do things you never did in the past.
* Pick up a sport or a hobby.
* Be open to learning new skills, trades, and ways of doing things.
* Consider taking online classes and learn how the latest technologies work.
* Subscribe to volunteering opportunities or involve yourself in a charity program that moves you.

My final word to you is this: *Your body is the temple of Christ; learn how to take care of it and reclaim your authority.*

In any and everything coming your way, remember that you are more than a conqueror and keep in mind that you need the right mindset to maintain your victory!

Fear is: **F**alse **E**vidence **A**ppearing **R**eal. On the other side of fear, there is a purpose! Take a leap of faith.

Soteria is a Greek word that means: to save or rescue. It is the same word that refers to salvation. The price was paid for us. And not only that, but it also gives us an inheritance, which is total wellness of being! We have a right to healing and deliverance of all the pain and hurt we have known because God loves us too much to see in bondage.

Small reminder

How to let go and break free from bondage?

* Seek God with all your heart.
* Identify the roots of your discomfort.
* Identify strongholds and cognitive distortion. (What are the lies I believe that are holding me back?)
* Decide to please God more than anything.
* Reform your way of thinking.
* Declare the Word of God over your life.
* Build a God-centered strategic plan.
* Disconnect yourself from anything, or anyone, toxic.
* Receive the right treatment (through counselling, prayer, etc.).

Let Us Pray!

*Father, we want to thank You for your love and compassion
toward us. Thank You for your salvation and the restoration
You are operating in us. Thank You for the big plans
You have for our lives, plans to prosper us, and not harm us.
Preserve and guide us through our wellness journey. Please
help us be obedient to Your will and ways.
To You be the glory, honor, and praise.
It is in the mighty name of Jesus Christ we pray.
Amen*

Meditation Verses

The Bible tells us:

2 Corinthians 3:17 (NIV)

Now the Lord is the Spirit, and where the Spirit of the Lord is, there is freedom.

Proverb 4:20-22 (NIV)

My son, pay attention to what I say; turn your ear to my words. Do not let them out of your sight, keep them within your heart; for they are life to those who find them and health to one's whole body.

Isaiah 26:3 (NKJV)

You will keep him in perfect peace, whose mind is stayed on You, because he trusts in You.

3 John 1:2 (NKJV)

Beloved, I pray that you may prosper in all things and be in health, just as your soul prospers.

1 Thessalonians 5:23 (NLT)

Now may the God of peace make you holy in every way and may your whole spirit and soul and body be kept blameless until our Lord Jesus Christ comes again.

Jeremiah 30:17 (NIV)

But I will restore you to health and heal your wounds,' declares the LORD, 'because you are called an outcast, Zion for whom no one cares.'

Colossians 2:9-10 (NLT)

For in Christ lives all the fullness of God in a human body. So you also are complete through your union with Christ, who is the head over every ruler and authority.

Wellness Plan Questions

1. What are your wellness goals?

_____

_____

_____

2. What do you need to achieve your goals?

_____

_____

_____

3. How will you achieve your goals?

_____

_____

_____

4. What are your indicators of success? How will you know you have achieved your goals?

_____

_____

_____

Notes

_____

_____

_____

_____

_____

_____

_____

_____

_____

_____

_____

_____

_____

_____

About the Author

Ketsia Morand is first and foremost a God fearing daughter, sister, wife, mother and friend. She believes that for everyone living and breathing, life is like a pendulum, continuously swinging from moments of highs and lows. It was from one of these temporary low moments Ketsia became highly interested and passionate about the human mind and well-being, both individually and how each relates to the other. Ketsia's interest led her to pursue a career in psychology.

She has devoted herself to helping others better navigate their lives by creating an organization that aims to integrate well-being at the physical, psychological, and spiritual levels.

Through her professional cognitive-behavioral life coach practice, Ketsia helps provide clients the tools they need to

achieve a perfect balance of the mind, body, and soul. Additionally, through her art, Ketsia uses her music to motivate and uplift people to a higher emotional and mental state. It is with great hope this book will help someone who is currently going through a low moment in their lives.

"May the favor of the Lord our God rest on us; establish the work of our hands for us—yes, establish the work of our hands."
—Psalms 90:17

Synopsis

Going through hardship, whether it's due to a breakup, grief, or any type of heartbreak, is never easy. And often, the hardships we face put up obstacles on the road toward our wellness journey.

Do you find yourself in an emotionally painful state where you feel there is no way out?

Do you find yourself stuck in the same compromising situations that you know are not right for you, yet don't know what to do?

Do you find yourself so overwhelmed by emotional pain to the point where you have lost all hope of one day feeling better?

If your answer is "yes," then this book is intended for you! Want to hear some good news? Your life doesn't have to be the way it has been! It is possible for you to heal. It is possible for you to feel good in your own skin, and yes, it is possible for you to get better!

When It Hurts Too Much To Let Go is for every person who has tried everything they could to heal emotionally without success.

This book combines the *why* and the *how* to let go, along with exercises that will help you convert your yearning for healing into concrete actions, solutions, and results.

Now is your time to heal, and you can start the journey right now.

Bibliography

American Psychology Association. "How to Choose a Psychologist," October 17, 2019. www.apa.org/helpcenter/choose-therapist.

Bourbeau, Lise. *Heal Your Wounds and Find Your True Self: Finally, a Book That Explains Why It's So Hard Being Yourself.* Lotus Press, 2002.

Brazelton, Katherine, and Shelley Leith. *Character Makeover: 40 Days with a Life Coach to Create the Best You.* Illustrated Edition. Zondervan, 2007.

Crozer Health. "PQRST Pain Assessment Method," April 28, 2021. www.crozerhealth.org/nurses/pqrst/.

McGraw, Phillip. *Life Strategies: The No-Nonsense Approach to Turning Your Life Around.* Ebury Publishing, 2007.

Siemer, Matthias, Iris Mauss, and James Gross. "Same Situation-Different Emotions: How Appraisals Shape Our Emotions." *Emotion (Washington, D.C.)* 7 (September 1, 2007): 592–600. https://doi.org/10.1037/1528-3542.7.3.592.

Strong, James, and W. E. Vine. *Strong's Concise Concordance & Vine's Concise Dictionary of the Bible: Two Bible Reference Classics in One Handy Volume.* Thomas Nelson, 1999.

Tan, Siang-Yang. *Counseling and Psychotherapy: A Christian Perspective.* Baker Academic, 2011.

Printed in Canada and the USA.

Printed in the USA
CPSIA information can be obtained
at www.ICGtesting.com
LVHW021541140824
788245LV00004B/423

9 781777 786502